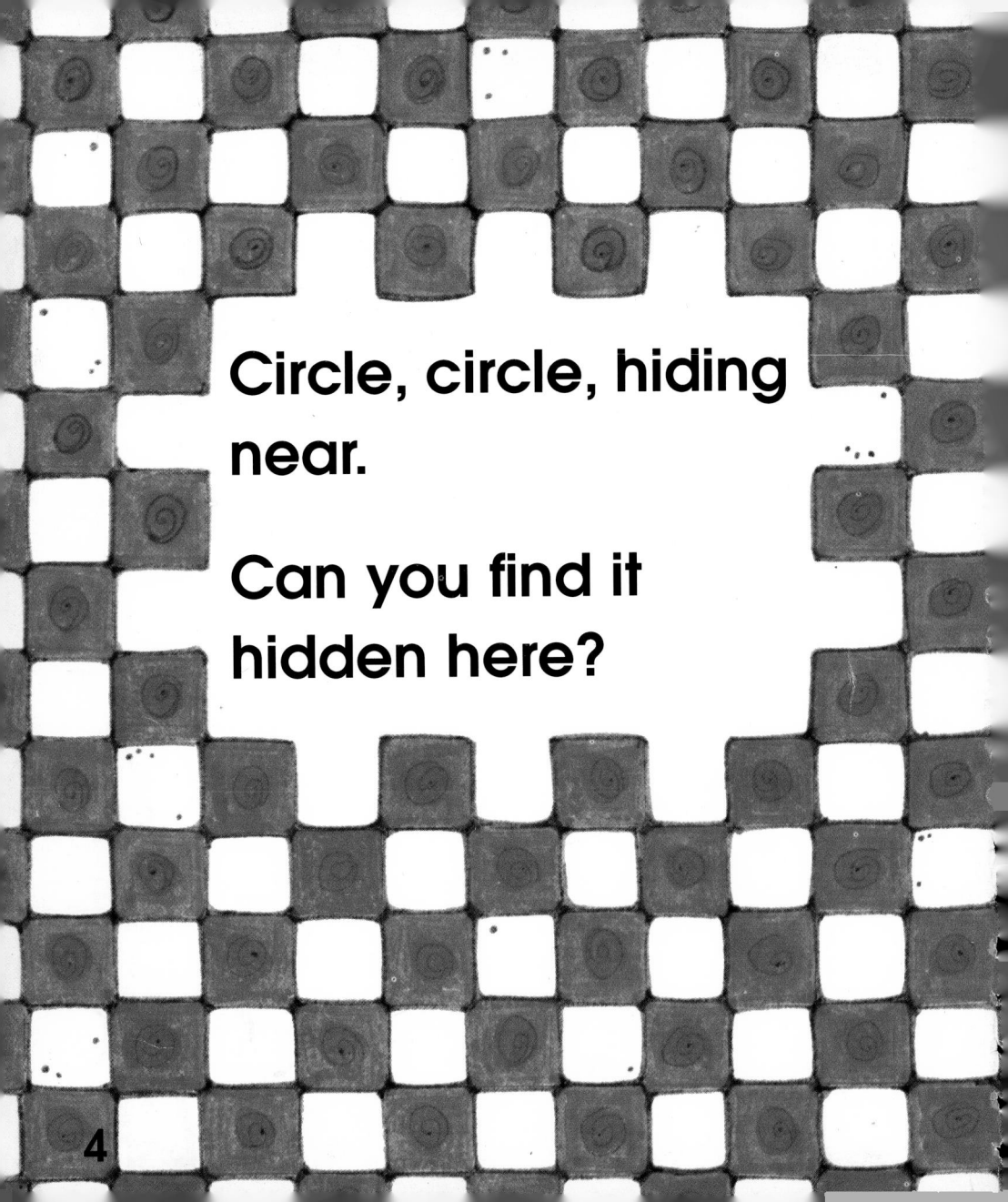

Circle, circle, hiding near.

Can you find it hidden here?

4

A PREDICTABLE WORD BOOK

SHAPES, SHAPES, ALL OVER THE PLACE

Story by Janie Spaht Gill, Ph.D.
Illustrations by Karen O.L. Morgan

 ARO PUBLISHING

SHAPES SHAPES ALL OVER THE PLACE

ISBN 0-89868-437-4–Library Bound
ISBN 0-89868-438-2–Soft Bound
ISBN 0-89868-439-0-Trade

5

Here it is! Did you
guess?

Turn the page and
find the rest.

7

Square, square,
hiding near.

Can you find it
hidden here?

9

Here it is! Did you guess?

Turn the page and find the rest.

10

11

Rectangle, rectangle,
hiding near.

Can you find it
hidden here?

12

13

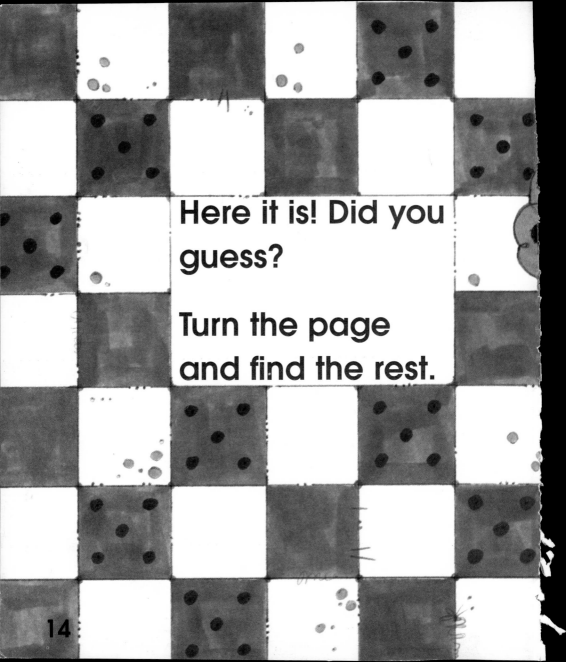

Here it is! Did you guess?

Turn the page and find the rest.

14

15

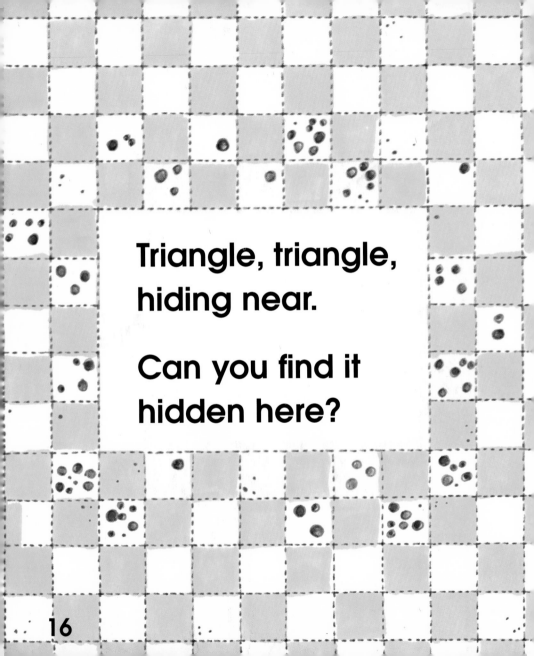

Triangle, triangle,
hiding near.

Can you find it
hidden here?

17

Here it is! Did you guess?

Turn the page and find the rest.

18

19

Oval, oval, hiding near.

Can you find it hidden here?

21

Here it is! Did you guess?

Turn the page and find the rest.

Once again the shapes appear. See if you can find them here.